THE PATH TO PROSPERITY

THE PATH TO PROSPERITY

Financial Strategies That Actually Work

B. VINCENT

QuantumQuill Press

CONTENTS

CHAPTER 1

Introduction

The author begins by discussing a life-centered approach towards money, which involves making different spending and saving decisions in order to eliminate debt and build savings. They suggest living more frugally without feeling deprived and having a long-term perspective when it comes to investing. These decisions may be unfamiliar and contrary to your current lifestyle. The main objective of this section is to make readers realize that the approach they have been following is flawed. The author uses the analogy of a woodcutter who is too busy cutting wood to sharpen their axe, resulting in slower progress. Similarly, many people work hard throughout their lives but fail to understand that making the right investments at the right time can make their journey easier. The introductory section explains how people have a misguided belief in the idea of working hard for money throughout their lives, which the author refers to as a money-centered approach towards life. This approach leaves individuals with little time to pursue their actual desires, leading to detrimental decisions and investments in search of short-term benefits. The core concept of this section is to encourage readers to break free from their habitual patterns, such as overspending, and focus on the common goal of achieving financial security. The entire book revolves around simple and conventional strategies for saving money by controlling expenses and investing wisely to ensure positive outcomes.

CHAPTER 2

Setting Financial Goals

I think that it is very important to know what you want to achieve in life and once you know what you want to do, it is also crucial to know how you are going to get there. When setting off on your trip, you have a destination in mind and very specific directions on how to get there. This is the same mindset you should have when planning your financial future. You'll need a definite something or somethings that you plan on working for and obtaining. You do not want to be vague about this. It will be very difficult to gauge your level of success in the future. A goal is something you desire that is currently out of your reach. This offers a sense of motivation and something to work for. Whether the goal is realistic or even attainable can be a vague question, and can depend on certain variables. A good way to gauge how realistic a goal may be is to base it off your potential in a certain interest and two thing tenure. If you need money to do something quick and current, short term goals could be 1-12 months in duration. If you need money for something that will take more than a year to attain, you have a long term goal. Throughout the entire process it is important to ask yourself if this goal is something that will better my current financial situation, and how this new achievement may affect future financial decisions. Your goal should also be specific and quantifiable. This makes it easier to measure your level of success upon reaching that goal. An example of a successful goal setting decision would be someone planning to invest in stock. A poor decision would be "I want to make money in the stock market." This is far too general and can be interpreted as someone with no set direction in trading trying to get rich quick. A goal for that same person that will offer a more sense of direction would be "I want to invest in long term bonds with a 20% return to increase my risk portfolio on current assets in the next 24 months."

2.1. Identifying Short-Term Goals

Set a specific amount for each goal and when you want to achieve it by. This will set the limits and will prevent the goal from being too easy and not challenging or too hard and unachievable. Make sure everyone involved knows and agrees on the goal to prevent conflict or much on it later down the track. For example, saving money for a holiday, the family needs to agree on a destination and how much money needs to be saved.

Financial goals allow you to prioritize and stay focused on what's important to you. A good example is that if you have high-interest debt, it's important to repay the debt before your retirement. Another reason is they give you a purpose and something to work towards. Reward yourself when you've achieved your goals, take pride in accomplishing it, and remember your goal to stop you from spending money on things that aren't important to you in the future.

Some of the reasons that short-term financial goals are important are: they give you direction, they provide a road map for the future, motivate you, and give you a sense of achievement.

2.2. Establishing Long-Term Goals

After you've wrestled with these questions, the best way to set your long-term goals is to use the S.M.A.R.T. method; that is, make goals that are Specific, Measurable, Attainable, Realistic, and Time bound. An example of a long-term financial goal using this method would be 'I want to have a net worth of $1,000,000 by the time I am 40 years old'. This is a specific amount of money, and it is definitely measurable.

Depending on your age, this goal can be attainable and realistic for a lot of people. It is also time bound as net worth is defined as the value of all assets, minus the total of all liabilities. For example, if you are currently aged 30 with a house worth $300,000 with a mortgage of $200,000, then currently your net worth is $100,000. This example would mean increasing your net worth by $900,000 over a period of ten years. This would require an investment of at least $90,000 a year, in order to achieve a 10% return (which is definitely possible by investing in various stocks or other investment vehicles). So you can see that by using the SMART method, you can derive long-term goals that provide you with a clear target to aim for, and with a realistic and specific plan on how to achieve it.

Long term goals are set to be accomplished over an extended period of time, typically over a year or more. The process of establishing long-term goals starts from your thought process. To do this, you need to ask yourself a series of questions, such as where you want to be in five or ten years. What sort of lifestyle do you want to have? Do you want to have your own business or invest in various things, such as stocks or real estate? What level of income will you need to sustain this lifestyle? When you are setting long-term goals, you need to be very specific.

CHAPTER 3

Budgeting and Expense Tracking

Creating a personal budget describes how to create a personal budget from scratch and why it is a crucial part of a successful financial plan. The author introduces readers to the four habits of successfully managing money: knowing exactly how much you spend, saving receipts, paying all bills on fixed dates throughout the month, and investigating all the specific ways to save. These habits are explained as a solid foundation for a simple yet effective budget. As with any plan to succeed, it is essential to set specific goals and put them in writing, and a personal budget is no different. Readers are shown how to powerfully achieve their dreams and financial goals with the use of a simple tool called the Money Map. This is one of the most unique and important features of this section as it introduces some highly valuable theory and practice in relation to managing money. The author not only summarizes the requirements of a written goal but also the money map and shows exactly how it is to be done. The remainder of the chapter walks the reader through the fundamental mechanics of a personal budget, firstly with how to analyze income and expenses and then how to categorize and calculate. Tracking expenses effectively is a review of the human tendency to believe that something is not as bad as it seems and how it leads to failure in managing money. It implies that tracking expenses is almost as important as money management itself and shows the reader how to concretize their decisions and visions into reality. By writing down estimated and actual expenses from the budget created earlier, readers can make a direct comparison and see if their money is going where they intended it to. If the reader is unable to make a positive comparison, the chapter lists the various ways to increase the tracking of expenses, such as using a small notebook, etc. Although it may seem tedious, the benefits that can be gained from the increased ability to track expenses can be quite profound. This section is concluded by showing how easy it is to do using modern technology and the potentially powerful tools of expense tracking software.

3.1. Creating a Personal Budget

The ZBB method: Zero-based budgeting is a technique that has been recommended by many personal finance gurus, perhaps most notably Dave Ramsey. With ZBB, your income minus your expenses equals zero. Every dollar is given a job. Since this method is quite involved and requires a full restructuring of your thought patterns concerning money, it may not be ideal for everyone. However, it is an excellent exercise in conscious spending and is worth trying at least once. In order to implement ZBB, you will need to know exactly where every dollar is going. Generally, this will mean tracking cash expenditures as well as using only cash for a month or two and tracking expenses with a debit card. Next, allocate your income into various categories, beginning with fixed expenses such as housing and insurance, then discretionary expenses such as entertainment and dining out, and finally savings. Adjust your allotments until you end up at $0. With ZBB, it is beneficial to set specific short-term savings goals, such as a vacation or a flat-screen TV. This gives every dollar a specific job and is more rewarding than the "save it because it's good for you" mentality.

The GI/GF method: This is a straightforward approach that works well for those with stable income. The idea is to budget your expenses around your net income. First, list your monthly income. If you are salaried, this should be relatively simple. If you are self-employed, an independent contractor, or your income varies, you may want to base your budget on your average monthly income. Next, list your monthly expenses. This should be relatively simple as well. Finally, subtract expenses from income. The goal is to have a little money left over. If you end up with a negative number, or no number at all, you need to reevaluate your spending habits.

To make more conscious and meaningful financial decisions, you need a clear, realistic understanding of your financial situation. The best way to develop that understanding is by creating a personal budget. The way you develop your budget is not important. What is important is that you have an accurate representation of your current financial situation and a realistic plan to guide your spending decisions. Here are some broad guidelines that you can tailor to fit your personal style.

3.2. Tracking Expenses Effectively

It is much less important how you track your expenses than that you track your expenses. The process of writing down every expenditure will cause you to question each purchase and will make it clear that many expenditures are out of all proportion to the joy that purchase brings. If you examine your expense book to find how much you have spent during the past year for presents, you will be surprised and perhaps chagrined to learn that the total is much larger than you supposed. And you will probably realize that much of the money has not been very well spent. If you are making good money now, figure how long it took you to produce the money that you just spent to realize how precious is the article purchased. There are innumerable ways to keep accounts. We can only point out what seem to be the best methods. A good many people keep the bills which they receive and at the end of the month make up from them, more or less accurately, a statement of their expenses. This method is very unsatisfactory because the money received is often an uncertain indication of what has been spent, and it is always apt to be forgotten which of the bills have been entered and which have not. Some sort the bills into their various kinds and add up the items of expenditure, making the monthly statement as aforesaid. This is better than the previous method but is still muy or less unsatisfactory.

CHAPTER 4

Saving and Investing

With saving, there is no risk in the amount that you first started putting into it, with interest then adding to the total amount of money saved. Usually, investment is more short term than saving, with many investments lying just around the year mark. This is why it is important to have a substantial amount of money saved up before looking into investing, as you do not want to be forced to cash in an investment early due to sudden unexpected financial requirements.

Investing is the purchase of an asset with the hope it will increase its value return over time. Often, investment involves the commitment of money or capital to purchase financial instruments or assets to gain profitable returns in the form of interest, income, or appreciation of value. What makes it different from outright saving is the risk and reward. Ideally, you want your investment to have a high rate of return, but without subjecting it to high risk levels. High return rates investments often involve the gamble of losing a lot or ending up with much less than what you started with.

In contrast to spending and borrowing, saving and investing, in a sense, are both forms of deferred consumption. Instead of using resources to meet immediate needs, you set aside income to meet future requirements. Saving is putting money aside a little at a time. When you save, you put your money into an account at a bank or other financial institution to be used at a later date. There are three key elements to successful saving: putting money aside regularly, using an account with a higher interest rate, and avoiding unnecessary risk.

4.1. Building an Emergency Fund

Typical recommendations range from $1000 to three months worth of expenses to 6 months of income. It should be saved in a readily accessible account. Since the purpose of this money is to provide a safety net during a difficult time, it should not be put into an investment where it could lose value or take a significant amount of time to liquidate. With the low interest rates of savings accounts, it might make sense to open an account with a higher yield, money market, or CD account. Although these might not be as easily accessible, they are still a better option than having to take on debt to finance your emergency.

An emergency fund is your insurance against these types of situations. The amount you should save depends on your family's situation. Two income families living on a strict budget can survive with a smaller fund because it would be easier for one spouse to find another job. On the other hand, families with one income earner or families with special needs children should aim to save a larger cushion.

When you least expect it, your financial position can take a turn for the worse. An unexpected layoff, a hospital visit, or a car accident can send your family into a financial tailspin. Without an emergency fund in place, you'll need to finance these sudden expenses with credit cards or loans. This debt can start a vicious cycle of increasing debt, high interest rates, and lowered credit worthiness, all of which can take years to repair. All the while, you'll be working simply to pay off debt instead of saving money to further your family's goals.

4.2. Exploring Investment Options

Investments can be a useful way to build your financial security. The Malaysian youth is progressively taking an interest in investments and are constantly seeking information and knowledge to better their understanding as well as the different types of investments available in

Malaysia. Investments play a crucial role for one to retire comfortably and is a sure means to provide a better quality of life. There are many different types of investments available to young people today. It is important to note that different investment schemes have different levels of risk and return. Although some might think it premature, young people can certainly entertain high-risk investments because they have a longer investment time horizon. An increase in the number of years for investment can enable an investor to take on more investment risk and the potential reward actually increases the longer one's investment time horizon, regardless of chronological age, due to the compounding effect. Essentially, a young investor has more to gain, and less to lose. That being said, investments should be easily liquidated should money be required urgently.

4.3. Diversifying Your Portfolio

By diversifying investment into different areas, this risk can be minimized. Investment can be spread into bonds, property, and shares in different industry sectors both locally and internationally. The idea here is that if one area of investment performs poorly, losses can be offset by the other areas which are performing well. Diversification can take a lot of time and effort, but it is well worth it in the long run.

It is a fairly simple concept: For all of us, our primary goal when investing is to gain the best return for the lowest risk possible. Would you knowingly risk losing everything you've invested? The answer would be a definite no. By placing all your money into one investment vehicle, such as company shares, you significantly increase the chance of losing the money you have invested. This is because the risk is not spread. If that company were to go out of business, you would lose all your investment. This is what transpired to Enron shareholders. The outcome from the Enron disaster was employees having invested their entire pension schemes into company shares. The value of those shares soon dropped to nothing and employees were left with no pension and no job.

It's quite normal to be concerned and confused about investing money in stocks and shares. With horror stories about average people losing half their life savings in weeks, who wouldn't be terrified? What many individuals fail to understand is our innate obsession and need to "put all our eggs in one basket." This is usually a grave mistake when it comes to investing our money.

CHAPTER 5

Managing Debt

It is important to consolidate all information on debt into a clear pile in order to establish where you want to be and what you want to be able to do in the future. This way, you have an end goal to work towards. With the client's vision of their end goal for the future in mind, they are asked if it would be difficult living off 70% of their current income to enable them to use 30% to pay off all debts in 3-5 years. Usually, it is not a difficult lifestyle adjustment, and it paints a picture to the client of being debt-free and having 100% income for their wants and needs. This is a solid debt repayment goal.

Good debt comes in the form of investing in something that will appreciate in value, has long-term benefits that outweigh the costs, such as tertiary education, or debts that have tax advantages. Sometimes, a home loan falls into this category. Bad debt, on the other hand, is the kind of debt that clients would like to get rid of. It tends to have higher interest rates with no tax benefits and is used to finance things which will have no lasting value. An example of this would be using credit to purchase household items or a holiday.

In order to make financial decisions that will start them on a path to greater prosperity, it is not unusual for clients to want to extend their reach and try their hand at investing. However, they wish to do so without increasing their level of debt. The first step in a debt management plan is to have a clear understanding of the different types of debt.

5.1. Understanding Different Types of Debt

Example 5.1.1: Bill takes out an auto loan of $20,000 with the car as collateral. The loan agreement is for 3 years and carries an interest rate of 6% on a reducing balance. In the second year of the loan, Bill is temporarily unable to work due to a medical condition and cannot afford the loan payments. The creditor repossesses the car and sells it at an auction for $17,000. Bill pays all remaining loan payments with some help from the additional $3,000 that he had in his savings account. The relative cost of the debt is relatively low because the creditor was able to recover most of the loan amount.

Secured Debt: Debts that are secured by an asset (also known as collateral) of some kind are categorized as secured debts. The creditor has the right to repossess or force sale of the asset in the event that the borrower does not fulfill the terms of the loan agreement. The relative cost of the debt is the degree to which the creditor can recover the amount of the loan in the event that the borrower defaults on the loan agreement compared to the value of the asset. The more likely it is that the creditor can recover or exceed the amount of the loan, the lower the relative cost of the debt.

In understanding different debt types and their relative cost, list your debts in descending order from the highest cost to the lowest. Then, categorize your debt as secured or unsecured. Finally, within each category, list the debts again in descending order from the highest relative cost to the lowest. Here's how to identify and categorize your debts.

5.2. Developing a Debt Repayment Plan

At first it may not seem as though what you are doing is having much of an impact on your financial situation. However, given enough time results are almost always guaranteed. As debts begin to disappear you will find it easier to allocate funds to the next debt on the list. This snowball effect will increase your confidence and rates of success in accomplishing the ultimate goal of becoming and staying debt free.

- Expedite the process: Sometimes additional part time work or a temporary increase in effort toward a career which includes up on sales commissions can be a quick way to generate cash to pay off debts. This will also eliminate idle time/money which might be spent in activities increasing debts and the interest on them.

- Timing: Set a goal or timeline to eliminate debts. Adjust spending habits to help meet this goal. Track your progress by keeping an updated amortization schedule.

- Consider balance transfers or debt consolidation: If you have equity in real estate and the discipline to avoid running up additional debt, borrowing against your home at a lower interest rate in order to pay off consumer debts can be a good long term strategy. However, this does carry some risk as you are transferring unsecured debt to debt which is secured by your home. Failure to make payments could place your home in jeopardy. An easier and less risky approach might be to simply transfer high interest credit card balances to lower interest credit cards. Keep an eye on transfer fees here, as these can offset any potential savings.

- Allocate extra money to debts: Credit cards usually have the highest interest rates, thus it is most beneficial to pay these off first. List debts in descending order from highest interest rate to lowest. Pay only the minimum on all debts with the exception of the highest. Budget money to contribute to paying this debt off as quickly as possible, without neglecting to make timely payments on other bills. Any additional funds should be used to pay off this debt, before moving on to the next highest interest. This process will save the most money in the long run.

Your goal in the plan phase of your project is to lead your team in determining the best approach for paying off debt. This will include allocating additional money to debts, identifying a timeline in which to become debt free, and considering some less orthodox methods for expediting the process. Generally, the primary focus should be paying off consumer debts such as credit cards which typically carry exorbitant interest rates. The more you can distinguish between past and future debts in terms of paying off the principal versus interest, the more progress you will feel that you are making toward the goal of becoming debt free. The following steps serve as a guide in determining the best approach for debt repayment.

CHAPTER 6

Creating Multiple Income Streams

Or you could start investing in rental properties. Ok, I know rental properties definitely do not sound simple, but they are a wise investment, especially in the long run. If you decide to start on this, you must research to make sure that this is something you are willing to put the time and money into. This is a prime example of a long-term investment, as the money invested from purchasing the property will gradually return and create more profit for you. This would be a second income stream, as the rent money you attain would be separate from the money you gain from your job.

It is quite simple. The more money you have, the more money you can save and invest. To create multiple income streams, one must have patience and keep the long-term in mind. The problem with most individuals is that when they think of increasing their income, they think of saving money from their 9-5 job. Their job is only one income stream, only one source of money. To start, think of having businesses that run without your active participation. This could include any type of small business. You could be selling goods on eBay. This could range from laptops to old clothes. You would be surprised at how much you can make from selling things that you no longer need.

Studies show that the wealthiest people have an average of seven streams of income. What? Yes, seven. I can imagine you must be thinking, how is that possible? That's because the wealthy know that you don't just have a job to make money. If you want to achieve financial abundance, you need to create multiple income streams. Having multiple income streams is the surest way to amass a fortune, and it puts you in a better position to deal with financial changes and crises.

6.1. Exploring Side Hustle Opportunities

Before jumping into the different side hustle options, the first step in finding an appropriate side hustle is to sit down and identify what you're trying to achieve. This might be to save for a holiday, pay off debt quicker, or simply increase monthly income. Knowing this will help set a gauge on how much money is desired each week, fortnight, or month, and whether what the person is doing is actually worth the time and effort. A good way to work out whether a side hustle is financially viable is to calculate how much you'll earn per hour. Some opportunities may sound great but may not be realistic in terms of how long it takes to earn the money. For example, an extra $40 a week sounds good, but if it takes 20 hours to earn it, is it really worth it?

When it comes to finding a side hustle, many people don't know where to start looking or what would be the best fit for them to earn the most money. This article will go through different options and the best approach to finding a suitable side hustle that's in line with the individual's skills and attributes.

Opportunities to make extra money through side hustles come in many shapes and forms. Think of a side hustle as another form of employment, but one that provides more flexibility and freedom. Many people probably don't think of side hustles as income-generating options that can impact their financial situation, and that they're just an easy way to make quick cash. While quick cash is a common result, there are hundreds of different ways side hustles can be used to seriously increase income over a prolonged period of time. Side hustles can be everything from a part-time job, something that someone is self-employed at, or something that just brings in extra cash for a short-term project.

6.2. Leveraging Passive Income Sources

Increasingly, new methods of leveraging today's technology thought up by individuals have disrupted ways of creating passive income. The implementation of these methods is limited only by the individual's imagination. These methods are not going to be described here because within the scope of your imagination and the freedom obtained from financial freedom is so wide that there will not be a right answer; there will only be an answer that is right to you.

It is very important to have some form of passive income mixed in with your active income to help make the transition to becoming financially free sooner than later. A prolonged absence of passive income will not provide a good transition in leaving the rat race. If the only income you have is the one you work for, you are in no better position than the next person who is unemployed and depending on a steady flow of capital via government aid. This simply does not equate to an existence of financial comfort.

Passive income is income that requires minimal effort to earn and maintain. Often times, it is referred to as progressive passive income when it steps a little up ahead of inflation. The definition of passive income is usually used in juxtaposition with active income, which is defined as linear and requires constant effort to maintain or create. The trouble with nothing is that it takes a long time to do. This is the greatest premise of creating multiple income streams. Often times, a quicker way to financial freedom can be obtained through graduating into higher-paying active income functions that also cross over into passive income, which is derived while the individual sleeps.

CHAPTER 7

Financial Education and Literacy

Economic conditions and trends in the global economy have a profound impact on individual financial situations. Knowledge of various economic indicators can inform consumers of the health of the economy and how it might affect their employment, income, credit patterns, and overall quality of living. Recognizing an economic problem early on is key to avoiding detrimental changes in financial plans and goals. Alternatively, an understanding of positive economic conditions can help consumers to capitalize on opportunities to advance their current situation. In any case, a clear understanding of the economy and how it affects personal financial well-being can act as a tool for decision-making and provide a rationale for future referral. Step one in this process, however, is to develop the knowledge and comprehension necessary to understand the economy, and build upon that base over time.

A solid education in finance is a good start, but in order to achieve long-term prosperity and security, it is no secret that consumers need to be able to apply what they have learned. Whether you are preparing to purchase a home, start a family, or invest in your future, it is essential that the financial decisions you make from day to day are based on a solid understanding of various economic conditions and options. Consumers who understand the key elements of the economy and its relationship to their personal situation are better equipped to weather changes in economic conditions and take advantage of various opportunities as they arise. This can be especially helpful for retirement saving, which is addressed in the next chapter.

7.1. Expanding Your Financial Knowledge

Remember that the more effort you put into increasing your financial literacy, the easier all this becomes. What was once hard to understand becomes second nature, and as you start to really understand financial systems and markets, your abilities to predict and make sound decisions will be greatly enhanced.

One of the best ways to learn about finance is to read material and then discuss it with like-minded individuals. Creating discussion often opens up new ideas and different ways of looking at things that you may not have considered before. Two heads are better than one, and applying this to a finance topic can lead to very efficient learning. An example would be joining an investment club or a finance forum.

With all the information that is out there, it's important to realize that not all of it is good quality. There is a lot of personal opinion that is stated as fact, and old information recycled as new information. Therefore, it's best to seek advanced-level material, as this is often subject to less distortion. Also, before using a strategy that you've read about, consider 'back-testing' it using historical data. This involves pretending that you are using the strategy to invest money in the past and seeing what results it would have produced. If you stick to this method, you will avoid new untested strategies of which the long-run results are unpredictable.

When it comes to expanding your financial knowledge, your goal is to understand a lot of the 'what' and 'why' behind the financial strategies that you hear about. Good sources of information to help increase your understanding include financial news websites, business news channels, financial and business newspapers, and best of all, books. A lot of business and finance books are written by people who have been there and done that and are willing to share the successes and failures. These are often the best learning tools as you get to learn from real-life experiences of others. When learning about investment, look for information that helps you understand the logic behind the investment strategy, not just the strategy itself. The better understanding you have of why a strategy works, the more likely it is you'll stick with it through the tough times.

7.2. Staying Informed about Economic Trends

"I need to stay one step ahead of those trends. That's why it's so important to be financially literate in this fast-changing global economy." Ed and his wife, Anna, understand this all too well. The Abbott family migrated to New Zealand and then to Australia in search of an improved lifestyle. After living in Sydney for 18 months, Ed was offered a job in yet another country, Singapore. Although Singapore offered better career prospects than Australia, the decision to move was difficult because Anna had just found out she was pregnant. Sorting through this confusion, the Abbotts realized that they were encountering the same situation that Ed's parents had over 25 years ago. At that time, Ed's parents had migrated from England to Australia in search of better opportunities. However, the decision to migrate was made just as Ed's mother had found out she was pregnant. This decision had a profound effect on the family's future, as Ed's father left a well-paying job and comfortable lifestyle to start again in a new country. In hindsight, Ed believes that had his parents seen the global economic conditions and future trends at that time, they may have decided against migrating to Australia and thus changed the course of Ed's life. From this experience, the Abbotts acknowledged the importance of seeing future economic conditions and trends and how they can affect individual lifestyles. Realizing that the average person has limited time and channels to gather economic information, the Abbotts decided to seek out professional advice in this area. Over a two-year period, with the help of a financial consultant, the Abbotts developed an understanding of how economic trends affect various investment markets and ultimately individual costs of living. This knowledge enabled the Abbotts to make more informed decisions with their remaining assets in Australia and future income in Singapore.

CHAPTER 8

Protecting Your Wealth

Protection is a proactive and reactive process. On the proactive side, it is important to live in a manner that is not excessively risky. For the most part, risks translate to things that can cost you money. There is a strong association between addictive behavior and lower income. Other risky behaviors include dangerous hobbies or sports and excessive debt. The single greatest thing you can do to avoid risky behavior is to educate yourself on what it will cost you in the long run. This is by no means to say that all recreation is bad. But it is important to weigh the benefits and costs of recreational activities. A cost that can wipe a person out is that of a lawsuit. A liability issue is a potential risk to income and assets. Liability insurance can often be procured to protect against this kind of risk.

It is often said that a good offense is the best defense. This is certainly true in the world of personal finance. The ability to generate a high income is not the primary determinant of financial success. Financial success is predicated upon the ability to keep what you earn. Most books on the topic of personal finance focus their efforts on increasing income. "The Path to Prosperity" differs from the competition. The book aims to increase your net worth. Protection of income and assets is the most critical component to lasting financial success.

8.1. Assessing Insurance Needs

You need to evaluate your insurance needs from the probability and severity standpoint. If the probability of an event is so low that the expense of insuring against it is greater than the expected loss, the event is not worth insuring. However, the measure of probability is contingent on the personality and individual circumstances of the person. If you would be devastated by events that have a low probability, you might need insurance with an aggregate expense greater than the expected loss. The severity stands for the size of the potential loss. In the case of an event that damages half of a $100,000 house, there is very little apparent need to insure the structure. On the other hand, a person with a $100,000 mortgage might find it necessary to insure the home against the event, because they have no cash with which to repair or replace the home. In general, insurance should only be purchased if you can reduce the probability times the potential loss amount of the event to a value less than you can afford to lose. It is important that you avoid over-insuring or duplicate insuring. Over-insuring is a waste of money and adverse selection due to moral hazard results in a sub-optimal allocation of resources into risk taking and prevention. Suppose that a family buys a life insurance policy on the father for $1,000,000 when in fact the father is worth more dead than alive (because of the $1,000,000 policy) to the insurance company. Due to the adverse selection, the father will take more risk and/or take less preventative measures than he would have without the policy, and the probability of his death will increase. The policy is also inefficient because the extra premium for the higher risk insured is the same as the expected increase in loss. Thus the family is paying $1,000,000 for the same expected loss for the father. Duplicate insurance occurs when the same item or risk is insured by two or more policies. Consider auto insurance that provides coverage for a rented car when the person has a personal auto policy with the same coverage. It is more efficient for the person to purchase a policy rider that covers rental cars as there will be an elimination or non-renewal of the redundant policy in which case there is a transfer of the duplicate premium to another more needed policy.

8.2. Estate Planning and Wealth Preservation

An advance in medical directive or living will effectively states to the courts and your physicians what kind of life-sustaining treatment you would like to be implemented if there is no reasonable chance of recovery from a life-threatening illness or injury. Finally, for single persons or widows, a do not resuscitate (DNR) notification can be placed in one's medical records and indicates that you do not wish to be revived in the event of cardiopulmonary arrest.

Various forms of power of attorney are available and are always worthwhile tools as they allow a designated person to manage your affairs if you are unable to do so. A guardianship/conservatorship (dependent on the state) also determines the affairs of an individual who is unable to do so but through the court system. This method is a last resort and should be avoided at all costs because of the legal fees that are likely to mount and the loss of control of one's affairs.

First is estate planning using a specialized advisor to prepare a will or trust. A will simply tells the world what you would like to do with your possessions upon your death. Trusts can also be used for this purpose but take more time to manage and are typically more geared towards wealth preservation. Both have their pros and cons. For example, a will has a better chance of withstanding legal action, but with probate and estate taxes, the beneficiaries could receive less than expected. With probate in some states taking two years on average, tying up assets worth 3-8% of the value and fees, many people will opt for a revocable living trust even though it does not protect against incompetency without enduring power of attorney or mental disability.

CHAPTER 9

Retirement Planning

The last calculation will generally just give you a total amount you need to save. What it does not factor in is the amount you could save through a tax-advantaged account. Depending on your tax bracket, contributing the amount saved in taxes through using a traditional account could cut as little as 75% of the needed savings amount. Conversely, with the beneficial tax-free withdrawals and no required minimum distribution in Roth IRAs and Roth designated accounts in employer-sponsored plans, saving the total amount can actually be less than what you would have otherwise spent using a normal taxable account. Now that we have a saving amount including tax considerations, all we need to do is ensure to find out the best way to save that money.

It would be wonderful if deciding how much we need to save for retirement was as simple as some general rule, such as saving ten times your yearly income. Unfortunately, guessing can lead to inadequacy in later years. However, there are helpful retirement calculators available on the internet, and the software commonly takes into consideration your current age, age at retirement, life expectancy, income, savings, Social Security benefits, and whether or not you have a pension plan. It then provides a total amount you need to save and a monthly savings amount. Other calculators simply require input of your current salary and age to suggest a savings path. Whichever method you choose, it is wise to revisit the calculation every few years to keep yourself account-able and aware of your increasing income and preparation, hopefully for at least partial early retirement.

9.1. Calculating Retirement Needs

3. It is highly recommended that you complete an Estimated Income and Spending Worksheet, as attempting to have less than 70-85% may just be wishing for a lower standard of living in an attempt to save less. Retirees are usually surprised to find that their expenses during retirement are generally higher than expected. Higher healthcare costs, increased leisure and recreational activities, home improvements, and possibly more spending on adult children can cause greater expenditure than when they were working.

2. Determine the amount of retirement savings that you would need to provide between 75% and 85% of your pre-retirement income, including the Social Security offset. Keep in mind you might need to aim higher than 85% if you have low income now and are trying to plan for retirement at around the same standard of living.

1. Find out what your estimated Social Security benefits will be. Estimate the benefit at three different levels of lifetime average earnings: $25,000, $35,000, and $45,000 a year. (These are 2009 amounts and are adjusted for inflation.)

Old methods of trying to figure out how much to save for retirement just won't cut it. A common guideline is that you'll need 70% of your annual pre-retirement income to live comfortably. However, this rule may not be effective, as some people may need 90% or more of their pre-retirement income, depending on their circumstances. To determine your retirement needs, you can also complete a more detailed estimate using the following approach.

9.2. Maximizing Retirement Contributions

When a person contributes a portion of their salary to a 401(k) retirement savings plan, that money is not subject to federal or state income tax. This means that the money is taken out of their gross pay, before federal and state income taxes are calculated and deducted. Assuming a 15% tax rate, if an individual contributes $100 to a retirement plan, that $100, the individual would have only received $85 had they taken the money as cash and paid taxes on it. So, the $100 contribution actually only costs them $85. The result is that the lower the individual's tax rate, the less it costs to save each dollar in a retirement plan. A person in the 15% tax bracket only has to save $85 to put away $100, whereas a person in the 28% bracket would have to save $72. In this case, it would be a good idea for the individual with a higher tax rate to increase the amount they contribute to their retirement plan, as it will effectively cost them less, because of the amount they save on taxes.

CHAPTER 10

Tax Planning Strategies

Warning: The following strategy is suitable for those with large consumer debts and the discipline to change their spending habits. This strategy is no excuse for a student to further finance his pizza and beer lifestyle. Step 1 in debt consolidation is to stop digging the hole. Step 2 is to use a home equity loan to pay off high-interest consumer debt and get a tax break in the process. This is because most interest paid on consumer debt is not tax-deductible, as consumer purchases provide no tax benefit to the economy. The interest on a home equity loan, however, up to $100,000, is tax-deductible, and in most cases, the interest rate is lower than the consumer debt. This strategy can save hundreds of dollars in tax and interest.

Understanding tax laws and benefits The implemented modification of the phrase from "Don't step over dollars to pick up dimes" is "Many individuals are stepping over hundreds of dollars to save a few". What this means is a lot of people are forgoing major tax deductions and credits simply because they are unaware of them. Because the tax legislation has been equated to an erosion of coral - slow and steady - it is easier to predict changes and plan to take advantage of them. Just to show how little tax knowledge the average American has, people actually take steps to ensure they are eligible for the earned income credit, not knowing that if this credit exceeds the tax owed, the excess can be received as a refund with their 1040 and a little schedule EIC. This occurs mostly because the credit is a phase-out credit and people aren't aware of it.

10.1. Understanding Tax Laws and Benefits

While it is beyond the scope of this article to provide an in-depth analysis of the tax code, there are several ways in which an understanding of tax laws and benefits can help you keep more of your money. The first is through taking adjustments to income. Adjustments to income enable you to directly subtract the amount of the expense from your income. The expenses are not required to exceed a certain percentage of your income as is the case with deductions. Thus, adjustments to income are generally more beneficial than deductions. A list of adjustments to income can be found in IRS Publication 17. It is important to always be aware of changes to the tax code that could make new expenses become deductible. One of the most important adjustments to income is saving money for retirement through an IRA. At moderate incomes, contributions to IRAs are able to be taken as an adjustment to income, thus enabling the saver to avoid paying taxes on that money. This enables savers to lower their tax rate and keep more of their money. At higher incomes, there are still opportunities to avoid taxes on money saved through retirement. Information on tax benefits for retirement saving using retirement programs sponsored by the employer can be found in IRS Publication 560, and it's quite possible that additional tax benefits from the later employer-sponsored programs could enable the saver to take the retirement savings contributions credit.

10.2. Utilizing Tax-Advantaged Accounts

Understanding that the accrued interest and growth of assets is tax-free, we devise ways to gain access to tax-advantaged accounts. This means that money that we place into these accounts and the growth that occurs with our contributions will be untaxed, given that we abide by the requirements and conditions of the specific type of account. Because the advantages of these accounts are void of taxation on interest and capital gains, these accounts outperform regular taxable bond and equity portfolios, assuming that the investor adheres to the constraints of the tax-advantaged accounts. The after-tax rate of return from taxable investments must always be compared against the after-tax rate of return of tax-free investments when deciding between the two. This can be observed through the equation: [(1-tax rate)(after-tax rate of return of taxable investment)] = (after-tax rate of return of tax-free investment) Given that the tax rate is not equal to zero, the right-hand side of the equation will always be positive, indicating that the tax-free investment offers a greater rate of return.

CHAPTER 11

Building a Strong Credit Score

Though building a strong credit score is not an overnight process, it is relatively simple. In order to build credit, you must have credit. This is accomplished by obtaining a line of credit. It is common for college students to apply for their first credit card in efforts to build credit. A student with no income and possibly no co-signer will more than likely secure a credit card with a high interest rate. This is acceptable, but a more reasonable approach, assuming the student has some income, would be to apply for a small loan at the local bank or credit union. Remember, credit cards and loans from smaller financial institutions usually have better rates. An additional tactic is to be placed as an authorized user on a parent's credit card. This will help to build your credit, but whether it will affect the primary cardholder in a positive or negative manner is dependent on their credit habits. An efficient way may be to use the card for some normal expenses and pay the bill. This expense is then repaid, therefore there is actually no debt. The card may later be fully paid off. Credit is built by good payment history, so this will have a positive effect. Any mistakes from the past can be rectified by obtaining a secured line of credit. This is done by depositing a certain amount with a financial institution. This amount will typically be the exact amount of credit. The credit is used normally (and monitored responsibly), and as the debt is paid off, the credit history is rebuilt.

11.1. Establishing Credit History

It's a tough fact to swallow, but you have to have credit to get credit. This is anxiety-provoking for many people who have heard horror stories about getting into credit card debt at an early age. But fear not. There are safe ways to ease into the world of credit, including college and secured credit cards. College credit cards often have low credit limits, and many companies target college students because they view students as long-term customers. Knowing that companies are looking to build brand loyalty, students can often find good deals with college credit cards. Many colleges have credit card companies come to the campus to offer information, thereby making it quite simple to apply. A secured credit card is another safe way to establish credit. These cards require that you make a deposit into a savings account as collateral. Your credit limit is based on the amount in your account. Shop around, as many secured credit cards offer terms almost as good as unsecured cards. Make sure that the card issuer reports to a credit bureau. If they don't, the card will not help you establish credit.

Credit, everyone wants it and mostly everyone needs it. Credit is hard to establish and harder to re-establish if something should go awry. In this chapter, we will cover ways to establish credit and things to avoid that may damage it, knowing the importance of a strong credit history. With determination and by carefully following the guidelines laid out in this chapter, you can save yourself a considerable amount of money in future loan costs by establishing a good credit record.

11.2. Managing Credit Responsibly

It is possible to develop and use credit in an acceptable way. Simply do the following: - Pay your bills on time - every time. One way to ensure that your bills are paid on time is to set up automatic payments from your bank account. - Accumulate a savings account. - Think long term. Before you purchase something on credit, ask yourself whether you will still be paying for it three years from now. - Do not rely on credit to bail you out of a poorly managed budget. - Examine your reasons for borrowing. Modifying your behavior may make borrowing unnecessary. - Pay off debts as quickly as possible. When the last payment is made on a car loan, consider making the same payment, but to yourself, into a savings account. This will build equity and lessen your dependence on credit when it comes time to replace your car.

CHAPTER 12

Navigating Economic Uncertainty

Strategy is the key word when it comes to facing economic uncertainty. You need to assess the situation rationally and make decisions on how best to secure your position. Knee-jerk reactions and quick fixes will rarely improve a situation, and can often make things worse. The aim is to adopt a flexible stance and work on reinforcing your safety net. What constitutes your safety net will differ from person to person, but the fundamental aim is to give yourself the best chance of maintaining your current lifestyle and avoid hardship, no matter what the future holds.

These are tough times. The economy is in recession and even though you haven't lost your job, you worry daily about your company's stability and your family's well-being. What can you do to make sure you can weather this storm? Economic uncertainty can be a terrifying prospect, but with careful planning you can make sure it doesn't spell disaster for you and your family.

12.1. Strategies for Financial Stability during Downturns

The importance of emergency funds is stressed throughout this book, and for good reason. During downturns, the probability of unexpected unemployment or underemployment increases, thereby making emergency funds an important tool for preventing a bad financial situation from turning into a disastrous one. Financial advisors or planners who are aligned with investment fund companies often tout the need to maintain investments to meet lavish retirement goals during economic downturns. The rationale behind this is that 'lost money' is only incurred when you sell off investments that are in a negative position. However, this line of thinking risks the need to incur loss by selling off investments when emergent financial needs are not met by the holder's current cash flow. Thus, it is highly recommended to save emergency funds in cash or cash-like instruments, such as short-term T-Bills. This strategy does not apply to those who are already in a high-paying secure career position.

Begin by deleveraging, or paying down as much debt as possible, such as credit card balances, mortgages, and auto loans, before the economic decline worsens. Minimizing your financial obligations now will help you keep your head above water when economic conditions worsen. If you have a strong balance sheet when entering a recession or depression, you will be better positioned to benefit from the economic opportunities that arise during downturns. This will help you move to the next strategy, which is to build up a sizeable amount of emergency funds.

12.2. Adapting to Changing Economic Conditions

As the economy moves out of a recession and into a recovery, some service and manufacturing industries will see increased business and profits. During a downturn, these companies will have streamlined their operations and reduced their costs. As the market strengthens, these firms will look to recapture or expand their market share. This could provide a very good investment opportunity into quality companies. An investor should look to purchase fractional ownership of a quality business (in the form of stocks) that is available at a good price. Identifying such an opportunity may be easier for those who have worked in a particular industry and have the knowledge to select winning companies. This tactic may also be employed by individuals seeking to switch careers or seeking higher-paying jobs in the same industry. They should invest time and money to increase their human capital, making themselves more attractive to employers. This too is an investment with potentially high return.

After implementing strategies to help weather the storm of a downturn, some positive changes can become habit and may even provide avenues for further growth and prosperity. As the economy improves, remaining frugal may mean a continued high level of savings. This is not a bad thing, and those who have managed to change their habits in such a way should not be quick to rush back into old, potentially harmful habits. Exercising discipline in spending and continuing to live within one's means (while saving the difference for future investments) will enable one to continue the process of saving and investing and may provide a large increase in net wealth over the long term.